Margaret Mead
World's Grandmother

Margaret Mead
World's Grandmother

by Ann and Charles Morse
illustrated by Harold Henriksen

Creative Education
Mankato, Minnesota 56001

Published by Creative Educational Society, Inc., 123 South Broad Street. Mankato. Minnesota 56001.
Copyright © 1975 by Creative Educational Society, Inc. International copyrights reserved in all countries.
No part of this book may be reproduced in any form without written permission from the publisher.
Printed in the United States.
Distributed by Childrens Press, 1224 West Van Buren Street, Chicago, Illinois 60607.
Library of Congress Number: 75-1343   ISBN 0-87191-425-5
Library of Congress Cataloging in Publication Data
Morse, Ann.   Margaret Mead, world's grandmother.
SUMMARY: A biography of the woman whose studies of primitive cultures
established her as one of the world's most acclaimed anthropologists.
1. Mead, Margaret, 1901- —Juvenile lit. [1. Mead, Margaret, 1901-   2. Anthropologists]
I. Morse, Charles, joint author.   II. Henriksen, Harold, ill.   III. Title.
GN21.M36M58   301.2'092'4 [B] [92] 75-1343
ISBN 0-87191-425-5

INTRODUCTION

Margaret Mead spends her life being curious about people. She studies people as children growing up, people getting married, having babies, becoming grandparents. Her kind of study is called anthropology. Her way of gaining information on the world's variety of people is by identifying with them and respecting them.

Margaret Mead, the renowned anthropologist, has traveled, observed, and taken notes and films of people in numerous cultures. She has written over twenty books and thousands of articles, and she has given hundreds of lectures every year. The peoples of the past, the youth of today, and the unborn generations of tomorrow are the message Margaret preaches. But the real message is Margaret Mead herself.

Margaret Mead World's Grandmother

"We are living in a world that no one has ever lived in before." Seventy-year-old Margaret Mead says that. And she says it often.

Margaret Mead is an anthropologist and a grandmother. Listening to Margaret Mead is like being inside a time-tunnel. She has gained wisdom from her age and experiences. She is continually changing her ideas in the light of today's discoveries, and she cares greatly for the unborn generations of tomorrow.

Margaret Mead is a granddaughter, mother, and grandmother. In herself, she keeps past, present, and future very much alive. She knows what she means by saying, "We are living in a world that no one has ever lived in before."

Through her long career, Margaret Mead has become a part of many different worlds — the world of an intellectually active family, the world of primitive cultures, and the world of advanced cultures. She has come to know the basic things people share. She has come to know many of the common problems people face. And she tells people what to do to help insure that the world will still be here for future generations.

Things change so fast in the modern world, Margaret Mead says, "that a person is born into one kind of world, grows up in another, and, by the time his children are growing up, lives still in a different world." This means that the children growing up today have to risk doing things their parents have never done. "Life in the twentieth century," she says, "is like a parachute jump. You have to get it right the first time."

Margaret Mead was born just as the twentieth century was being born — on December 16, 1901, to Emily Fogg Mead and Edward Sherwood Mead. She was the first of five children.

Margaret has frequently said of herself that she was a child that both her parents wanted. She had the traits that each parent liked in one another — Margaret had her father's mind and her mother's concerns. She was often told that everything about her was wonderful. That positive image stayed with Margaret as she grew up. Even as she lectures today, it is obvious that Margaret Mead knows that what she has to say is important.

Richard, who was born two years later, was the only son of the Meads. Still, Margaret's place in the family was never altered. It was always very clear to her that she was loved and cherished simply because she was herself. "There's no one like Margaret" was a phrase often heard around the Mead house.

Emily Mead kept notebooks on Margaret and Richard in which she carefully noted new words or interests each child displayed. As she raised her children, Mrs. Mead continued to study and pursue her own interests. In time, she secured a college degree.

Mrs. Mead always made sure that there was a variety of people visiting their home so that the children would be exposed to interesting people. Dinner table conversation might revolve around taxation or the feminist movement. Ideas were always in the air at Margaret's house, and Emily Mead made certain that the children's ideas were included in the conversations.

When Margaret was four, Katherine was born. She was a happy, responsive child, but, at just nine months, Katherine died. Margaret sensed that the tragedy touched her father most deeply. He never again felt that he could risk giving so much love to a child.

Two years later Elizabeth was born. Since she was a frail child, the family was concerned for her life. In her autobiography, *Blackberry Winter,* Margaret looked back on this time and explained the quiet confidence she had then. "I felt that she had been sent to take the place of the baby who had died. This feeling had a decisive effect on my life as it gave me an abiding faith that what was lost would be found again."

Elizabeth survived and was to become Margaret's favorite sister. Only a year and a half later, Priscilla was born.

From her father, Margaret learned very early about the world of professors and academic life. Mr. Mead taught economics at the University of Pennsylvania, and he was an editor of a weekly newspaper.

Edward Mead impressed Margaret with an intense interest in the way things were done, in the science of things.

She remembers that her father gave her much affection. It was from him that she learned the importance of thinking clearly. Her father would support her in any project if it would add even one small fact to the world's knowledge.

Margaret thrived in the challenging environment her parents provided for her. But it was her grandmother who was the biggest influence in her life. Margaret once said that the content of her conscience came from her mother's concern for other people and from her father's insistence on factual knowledge. But the strength of her conscience came from her firm and loving grandmother.

Grandmother Mead had gone to college, something unusual for a girl at that time. She married, had a child, and kept her career as a teacher. She convinced Margaret that there was nothing in life one couldn't do or understand. It is clear that Margaret's ability to jump into unknown worlds was inspired by her grandmother.

Margaret described her grandmother as the central figure in their house. Her room was always the best in the house — sunny, spacious, and equipped with a fireplace if possible.

Grandmother Mead spent much of her time being Margaret's teacher. She taught her algebra and botany. She would give Margaret a description of some plants and send her out into the woods to find samples. She encouraged Margaret to continue her mother's habit of observing and taking notes on her sisters. Margaret was told to listen to the children talk and then try to identify the source of new words in their vocabularies. If she heard one of the girls say that she felt "raggedy," Margaret would have to figure out that it probably

GRANDMOTHER

came from Riley's poem, "The Raggedy Man."

Besides teacher, Grandmother Mead was the family storyteller. She told stories that had a moral. She told funny stories, classic stories, educational stories. Best of all, she told stories from her past when she lived in the little town of Winchester, Ohio.

Margaret's grandmother always talked about people — not with a sense of gossip but with a sense of concern. Margaret often said that her grandmother gave her an extra century by sharing her past with her.

Margaret remembers spending almost all of her early childhood with her brother. She and Richard ate together, played together, and were even dressed alike. Richard was intensely loyal toward his sister, but he was frequently sick and could not play the way Margaret often wished he could. She longed for a mischievous older brother who would "be a ringleader in positive wickedness." To Margaret's delight, when she was 13, her cousin Philip came to live with the Meads for a couple of years. Philip knew exactly how to be naughty and so led Margaret into the kind of adventures she seemed to need to round out her childhood.

The Mead family moved often around the state of Pennsylvania in order to be near the various schools where Edward Mead taught. With the family's frequent moves and with Grandmother Mead taking care of much of Margaret's education, her schooling was unusual. Between the ages of five and 17, Margaret spent two years in kindergarten, one year — but only half days — in fourth grade, and six years in high school.

Emily Mead felt that each move had to bring new experiences. Margaret was born in Lansdowne. When they moved to Hammonton, she had carving lessons because the only artist in town was a skillful woodcarver.

The Meads lived two years in Swarthmore where Margaret learned to build a loom. She took painting lessons from a local artist in Bucks County and later in New Hope.

The home that stands out most in Margaret's memory was their farm in Buckingham Valley. The family moved to the 107-acre farm when Margaret was about ten.

The farm introduced the Mead children to the exquisite sights of wild flowers, and wheat fields and to the sounds of a brook running through a ravine. The farm excited the children with its three-storied barn where the loft was perfect for giving plays and the chutes were just right for sliding down in hide-and-go-seek games.

Horses, too, were a new experience for the Mead children. They were never allowed to ride them, but they learned to drive the horses from the buggy.

At 11, Margaret seemed to have time on her hands, so her parents finally decided to send her to school full time. She attended the Buckingham Friends Grade School, graduated in 1915, and went to the public high school the following year.

The next winter the Meads moved to Doylestown where Margaret attended a good small-town high school. Yet school held no challenge for Margaret.

She entered into every activity at school and made friends easily. But she was bored. So she took up writing. Margaret started writing a novel, wrote several school plays, and helped to start a school magazine.

Early in her school career, Margaret realized that she was different. She knew it was not because of any peculiar gift of her own but because of her unusual background. Margaret was often sensitive about being different, but she still kept her intense curiosities and interests.

Margaret graduated from Doylestown High School in June, 1918. Later that year her family moved to New Hope.

At this time, a financial crisis at home made Margaret's college career uncertain. Her father suggested she study nursing rather than try to attain a college degree. Margaret exploded in what she called "one of the few fits of feminist rage I have ever had."

Mrs. Mead succeeded in talking her husband into letting Margaret attend DePauw, the college Mr. Mead had attended.

Margaret planned for DePauw with much enthusiasm. Her home and her family had prepared her for this step into the academic world. Yet DePauw disappointed her. She spent the year being snubbed by sorority girls.

Still, Margaret learned from the experience. She began to see that both those who are rejected and those who reject suffer deep character damage. She saw that superior and inferior attitudes are not ways upon which to organize a society.

Margaret also learned from her experience at DePauw just what kind of college she did want to be part of. It should be an evironment where people were enthusiastic about ideas and issues, where people would stay up half the night talking, discussing, exchanging opinions. It should be a place where persons were respected the way they had always been at home.

Margaret found that place the next year in New York at Barnard College on the campus of Columbia University. There Margaret made life-long friends and joined a feminist group who vowed "never to break a date with a girl for a man." It was at Barnard that she discovered her career.

Senior year proved to be the turning point in the direction of Margaret's life. She wanted to make a contribution to one of the social sciences, but she didn't know which one. At that time, she had to choose between two of the most important courses open to seniors. She could take a course in psychology or a course in anthropology given by Dr. Franz Boas. Margaret chose anthropology.

Margaret's fundamental curiosity about the different peoples of the world influenced her choice. That choice gave direction to her life and eventually pointed her toward becoming one of the greatest anthropologists of the twentieth century.

Anthropology was not totally new to Margaret. Her parents had communicated to her a respect for all cultures. She had always been interested in the origin and destiny of people. But the world that Dr. Boas opened to Margaret led her to see the beginning, groping steps of mankind with a passion she had not yet experienced. Margaret soon became dedicated to studying people.

Dr. Boas also impressed Margaret and the other students with a sense of urgency about their study. He felt that anthropologists should develop an understanding of primitive cultures before they would become extinct.

At this time, Margaret was reading a book, *The Mystery of Easter Island,* in which the author sailed to the Island to gain information about some peculiar statues. When she arrived, the one person who knew about these statues was ill. He died shortly after the author arrived, and all the information died with him. Like Boas, Margaret became convinced that she must do her work among primitive people before valuable information was lost.

However, Margaret and Dr. Boas did not agree on where she should do her research work. He wanted her to study adolescent girls among American Indians. Margaret wanted to go to Polynesia and study culture change rather than adolescence.

Dr. Boas was a definite, no-nonsense man. Margaret was equally definite and firm. She had been fascinated by all that she had read of the mysterious people of Polynesia. She knew it was dangerous for a woman at that time to travel to the Polynesian Islands, but she felt that she could handle the problems.

Margaret suggested a compromise. She would be willing

17

to study the adolescent girl, but it had to be in Polynesia.

Margaret's father supported her. He felt that she should be allowed to explore the part of the world that interested her. He offered her a thousand dollars for the trip.

Finally, Dr. Boas agreed to let her go to the Polynesian Island of Samoa. Margaret was ecstatic. His decision made her realize that the freedom to work as one wished was extremely important.

Margaret was also quite aware of what she wanted to study and how she should go about it. She wanted to preserve in written form some of the aspects of primitive life styles before the societies disappeared forever. In Samoa, Margaret wanted to see how the adolescent girl spent her day, how she made friends, and whether she grew up with the same stress and strain as the American girl experienced.

The young anthropologist also knew that studying people presented problems. She wrote once, "We cannot point telescopes at human beings to watch them, nor could we put them all together in a giant glass jar to watch them as fruit flies are watched." She realized that she had to become a part of the community she was studying. "A man watching another man can understand something about how he feels; and if he learns the other man's language, he can ask him questions and listen to his answers."

It was early in October, 1925, when the small female anthropologist stepped off the boat in the little town of Pago Pago. Samoa, a tropical island in the South Seas, was 7,500 miles from Margaret's home. There was no one to meet her in Pago Pago. She felt very much alone.

Margaret's first challenge was to learn how to feel comfortable with the Samoan way of life. She learned to eat the food of the Samoans, sleep on their mats, learn their gestures, jokes, manners and customs.

The language was soft and free flowing and very difficult for Margaret to master. One day she found herself saying repeatedly under her breath, "I can't do it!" until she realized that she was saying, "I can't do it!" in Samoan. Margaret knew then that she could do it.

When the next boat came, Margaret was ready to leave Pago Pago for Tau, the village of the Turtle and the Shark. In Tau, she could establish a base for her field work. The village chief, Ufuti, had agreed to have her live at his house. His daughter, Fa'amotu, acquainted Margaret with many of the characteristics of the adolescent girl. Since Margaret was only five feet tall and 23 years old, it was easy for her to be identified with the girls she was studying.

The adolescent and pre-adolescent girls came day and night to the place where Margaret lived. Margaret would give the girls simple tests and learn of their backgrounds. From her findings she would work up case histories on the girls.

Margaret was never sure whether she was using the proper methods to complete her anthropological study. She wrote of her difficulties to Dr. Boas. He wrote back, assuring her that since there were no precedents to fall back on, she must be using adequate methods. His letter, however, arrived only after she had finished her work and was ready to leave the village of Tau.

After nine months of study, Margaret returned to New York and joined the staff of the American Museum of Natural History. There Margaret had a small office under the eaves, with a back stairway leading down from her office. She still has the office and says she likes having the back escape.

There in her top-floor office Margaret wrote her first book, one of her most popular ones, *Coming of Age in Samoa.* In it Margaret describes the peaceful way in which Samoan girls grow into adulthood. Her style is easy, sometimes even romantic, as she shows the calm life style apparent in the Samoan culture. The book became a best seller.

Just before her next field trip, Margaret married an anthropologist, Reo Fortune. They both sailed to the Admiralty Islands in New Guinea where they would study the Manus. Though they were a much more rigid people than the Samoans, Margaret greatly enjoyed the people. They, in turn, affectionately called her "Miss Markit Mit." Margaret's insights from this field trip were described in her second book, *Growing Up in New Guinea*.

Margaret Mead calls the next few years in her life "the years between field trips." She and Reo continued to work on their writings and made short field trips in the United States to study some aspects of Native Americans.

In December, 1931, Margaret and Reo returned to New Guinea. Margaret went to study three more tribes — the Arapesh, the Mundugumor, and the Tchambuli — in order to find out about the different ways each tribe expected its men and women to behave.

Margaret found the Arapesh people peaceful, congenial, and loving to their children. However, the Arapesh frustrated her. She could not uncover what she went to study. The Arapesh expected nothing different in the behavior of their men and women.

In August of 1932, Margaret and Reo left the Arapesh and went to study a cannibalistic tribe, the Mundugumor. While the Mundugumor were entirely different from the Arapesh, the study brought Margaret no further. The Mundugumor people believed all adults should be very aggressive. So here, too, there was little difference between men and women.

There were endless rivalries and severe dislike of children among the Mundugumor. "Women wanted sons and men wanted daughters, and babies of the wrong sex were tossed into the river, still alive," Margaret reported. Finally after three months, Margaret and Reo left the Mundugumor tribe.

It was early in 1933 when Margaret, Reo, and the English anthropologist, Gregory Bateson, teamed up in an "eight-foot square mosquito room" in the Tchambuli village. Here men and women were expected to behave differently.

At last, Margaret had found the missing piece in her study. Not only did the men and women act differently from one another, the Tchambuli acted differently from the men and women in America.

The Tchambuli women were hearty and businesslike as they managed the family valuables. The men arranged their hair in soft curls, carved wooden objects, painted, and gossiped. Margaret said of that culture: "Tchambuli is the only culture in which I have worked in which the small boys were not the most upcoming members of the community. . . . In Tchambuli it was the girls who were bright and free. . . ."

Working together among the Tchambuli, Margaret and Gregory began to see that they shared similar interests and concerns. So after Margaret left the New Guinea tribe of the Tchambuli, she and Reo decided to get a divorce. Early in 1936, on their way to a field trip among the Balinese, Margaret and Gregory Bateson were married.

Margaret was 34 and Gregory 31 at the time they began their trip to Bali, an island in the South Sea. "I had what amounted to a lifetime of completed work behind me,"

Margaret said. "Gregory had a lifetime of work . . . ahead of him. We looked about the same age. . . . But in many ways there was a tremendous difference between us. I had grown up at 11 and so had been grown up for over 20 years; Gregory kept his slight asthenic figure until the war ended, almost 10 years later."

Though each had a different purpose, Bali gave both Margaret and Gregory a chance to work in the way they wanted. Margaret wanted to work with a highly intellectual person and in a culture rich in ceremony. Gregory wanted to work with a new method — the camera — to speed up the process of his work.

Margaret and Gregory were among the first anthropologists to use still and motion pictures. Margaret also was one of the first to develop the study of semiotics, that is, the study of how people communicate through gestures.

Mosquitoes, heat, and the infections which characterized the islands of New Guinea were not at all missed by Margaret and Gregory as they enjoyed the beautifully terraced land of Bali. Gregory took over 25,000 photographs and thousands of feet of motion pictures, a giant stride for anthropology at that time. Margaret took up her study of the children within the total setting of their lives. Their secretary also took notes in Balinese so that they would be able to make vocabulary checks. Both Gregory and Margaret enjoyed the drama, music, and dance of the Bali ceremonies. To both of them, the Balinese were a treasure to study.

In all her field trips, Margaret Mead is able to get much information because of her uncanny way of identifying

immediately with the people she is studying. Her method is intuitive. She settles in with the people, eating rotten fish if necessary, to become like them.

Ken Heyman, who photographed with Margaret on several of her later trips, reported that he saw her sitting on the ground for hours at a time watching seemingly unimportant details. "She knows how to use her eyes — how to see," Heyman says.

Bali proved no exception. Margaret and Gregory amassed

an enormous amount of material in just two short years. It was exciting material.

Since studies in anthropology rely on comparison, Margaret and Gregory planned a large comparative study for the next three years. They hoped to get psychologists, scientists, physicians, and interpreters all to work in comparing the Balinese to other cultures. But there was one problem.

It was 1939. World War II became a reality, dashing their dreams of securing any more people for the project. Margaret and Gregory went back to New Guinea where they were both familiar enough with the culture to make some of the comparisons they needed.

However, Margaret felt that not enough results were gained from the trip to Bali. The field work in Bali was an intense, exhilarating time for both Margaret and Gregory. Margaret has made return trips to Bali for more photographs and has exhibited them. But the experience remains unsettled for her.

Later in 1939, Margaret Mead entered a totally new world. Earlier in her life she had been told that she would not be able to have a baby. She had had several miscarriages. Yet through these experiences, Margaret maintained a belief that she would one day have a child. On their way home from New Guinea to New York, Margaret discovered that she was pregnant. Once it was certain, Margaret took extreme cautions so that she would be able to carry the baby to birth.

Many people would simply have a baby. But Margaret Mead was very exact in planning every detail of the baby's arrival. She felt determined to keep this baby. She asked the now famous Dr. Benjamin Spock to be the pediatrician because she wanted a doctor who would be open to the way she wanted her baby cared for. She explained that she wanted him there at the birth so that he could take over immediately. She wanted a film made of the birth of the baby so that it could be referred to later with accuracy. She wanted to be able to nurse the baby whenever the baby seemed hungry.

All these requests were quite unheard of at that time. But Margaret Mead's reputation was well formed by then, and she received what she wanted.

Because of the war, Gregory Bateson had to return to England for military service. Margaret had to wait alone for the birth of their child.

She made a conscious effort not to think about what the baby would be like. She disciplined herself against hoping for either a boy or a girl; she wanted to keep an open mind. She did not want to have an image of what the child might look like or what gifts she might like the child to have. Margaret Mead has always felt that keeping an open mind makes it more possible for the child to be born into its own unique personality.

Mary Catherine Bateson was born on December 8, 1939. The birth was delayed ten minutes while the photographer dashed out to the store for flashbulbs.

Gregory was able to return from England shortly after his daughter was born. He and Margaret had decided that if they had a boy, they would move to England because they felt the English did a better job of bringing up a boy. If it were a girl, they would live in the United States where girls are better off.

From birth, Cathy (as they called her) was respected by her parents as a person with an identity of her own. "In my family," Margaret had said, "I was treated as a person. . . . It was never suggested that because I was a child I could not understand the world around me and respond to it responsibly and meaningfully."

Soon after Cathy was born, Margaret and Gregory gave up their apartment to live in a joint household with friends, Larry and Mary Frank. Gregory returned to England in 1944 where he wanted to continue his work. Margaret and Cathy continued to live with the Franks until 1955 when the house was sold.

While Cathy was a baby, Margaret worked part-time for the Museum of Natural History. Because of the war crisis, she became more involved in researching how the American people were facing the war.

As a result of her research, Margaret wrote *And Keep Your Powder Dry* which considered the qualities of the American character during a war. In the summer of 1945, Margaret began to write a sequel to that book. But when the atomic bomb exploded over Hiroshima and Nagasaki, Margaret tore up the manuscript. Once it was discovered that people could completely destroy the entire world, "every sentence was out of date," she said of her manuscript.

After the bombing it was a completely new world. Margaret felt that almost overnight everyone had become an immigrant to this new world.

The times brought personal changes for Margaret Mead.

She stopped doing field work and began working in collaboration with many people and in a variety of areas. Margaret began to turn the insights she had gained from her field trips toward a general study of contemporary cultures.

She taught anthropology and through the years received many speaking requests. She almost never gives the same lecture twice. Her subjects include: religion, race, family, hunger, women's careers, drugs — almost every phase of human life.

Margaret continued writing, and she often used her lectures as a way of clarifying her thoughts. After she had spoken to several groups, she would expound on those ideas in a major address or in a book.

Margaret's seven-and-a-half-hour conversation with James Baldwin was transcribed into a best seller, *A Rap on Race.* In it she and Baldwin both emerge as "disturbers of the peace," people unwilling to let the issues of the day slide past them.

In 1953 Margaret returned to Manus to record the dramatic postwar progress of the culture she had studied in 1932. In 1965 and 1966, she made other short trips to Manus, and in 1967 she helped to produce a 90-minute show for National Educational Television. The program, "Margaret Mead's New Guinea Journal," showed the marvelous strides the Manus had taken from almost stone age to the modern world.

Margaret Mead has been recognized by both the public and her colleagues for her brilliant study of people. She was named *Outstanding Woman of the Year in the Field of Science* by the Associated Press in 1949 and *One of the Outstanding*

Women of the Twentieth Century by Nationwide Women Editors in 1965. Margaret has also been president of the American Anthropological Association and the World Federation for Mental Health. On December 2, 1971, Margaret Mead received the Kalinga Prize, awarded by UNESCO, for her ability to interpret science to the public. She was Curator of Ethnology at the American Museum of Natural History until she retired in 1969.

Although she is officially retired, Margaret has stayed on in her office in the tower of the museum, maintaining a staff of nine assistants. She continues teaching anthropology, writing, and speaking on tour.

When Margaret Mead lectures, she presents a somewhat unassuming manner. Fluffy hair surrounds a very pleasant, unwrinkled face; her voice is homespun. But Margaret Mead can also present a very imposing figure in her flowing cape and her black, shoulder-high staff.

The staff was acquired when Margaret broke her ankle ten years ago and the doctor told her she should use a cane. Margaret rejected the idea of "looking old" as she stooped to use a cane; hence the tall staff. Though the English "thumb stick" sometimes presents problems as she enters elevators or cabs, it gains much attention for her when she waves it to gain recognition at a meeting.

At the overpopulation conference in Bucharest in 1974, much time was spent on all the problems facing a crowded world. At the end, the 73-year-old anthropologist, "the Grande Dame of the students of mankind," was called upon. Margaret Mead concluded the conference, "Oh, we can still do something — otherwise I wouldn't be here. I wouldn't make a profession of being a doom-watcher." As long as she's alive, Margaret Mead spreads hope.

Despite the numerous honors, awards, and recognition Margaret Mead has received, she still feels that one of the most exciting events that has happened to her was becoming a grandmother.

Margaret had often thought that her daughter Catherine and her husband, Barkev Kassarjian, were the kind of parents that a child might choose to have. She expressed strong feelings about giving children the freedom to choose their own path. "This sense that a child has somehow chosen its parents is a very deep and old human feeling. It gives a child a status as an individual in his own right."

Again, Margaret steeled herself against daydreaming about what her grandchild might be like. And again, Margaret's life was irreversibly changed. On October 9, 1969, Margaret Mead became a grandmother. "The birth of a child," she wrote after becoming a grandmother, "changes one's own place in the world and that of every member of a family in ways that cannot be completely foreseen."

Sevanne Margaret, whom they call "Vanni," was born on the day Margaret's book on the generation gap, *Culture and Commitment,* was going to press. Margaret dedicated the book to "my father's mother and my daughter's daughter."

As granddaughter, mother, and grandmother, Margaret Mead embodies in herself the message she teaches: to cherish the living, remember those who have gone before, and prepare a world for those who are not yet born.

Ann and Charles Morse

Charles and Ann Morse spend as much time as they can hiking and fishing with their children on their farm in Wisconsin. At other times, they write and design books and other educational materials at their home in Minneapolis. They call their business Guild House Associates and they call their farm Poche de la Paix, which means pocket of peace. Their daughter, Kristin, is artistic, and their son, Scotty, is musical. They are the two permanent children. Foster children have been known to live with them, too, for a year or two at a time. Ann swims, plays tennis and guitar. Charles enjoys crafts and carpentry — it's good he does because he's always fixing something.

Harold Henriksen

Harold was born in St. Paul, Minnesota and has lived there most of his life. He attended the School of the Associated Arts in St. Paul.

Even while serving in the Army, Harold continued to keep alive his desire to become an artist. In 1965 he was a winner in the All Army Art Contest.

After the Army, Harold returned to Minnesota where he worked for several art studios in the Minneapolis-St. Paul area. In 1967 he became an illustrator for one of the largest art studios in Minneapolis.

During 1971 Harold and his wife traveled to South America where he did on-the-spot drawings for a year. Harold, his wife and daughter Maria now live in Minneapolis where he works as a free lance illustrator.

close ups

Walt Disney
Bob Hope
Duke Ellington
Dwight Eisenhower
Coretta King
Pablo Picasso
Ralph Nader
Bill Cosby
Dag Hammarskjold
Sir Frederick Banting
Mark Twain
Beatrix Potter
Margaret Mead
Rose Kennedy
Walter Cronkite
Henry Kissinger